YUST *for* FUN

Norwegian-American
Dialect Monologues

By

ELEONORA *and* ETHEL OLSON

Introduction by Paul F. Anderson
Illustrations by Ruth Askegaard

First Printing 1925
Second Printing 1929

Minneapolis, Minnesota
ISBN: 0-9602914-1-5

VICTOR RECORDS

BY

Ethel and Eleonora Olson

(10-inch: list price 75c.)

Record No.	Title	Artist
72060	Norsk Kvinde i telefonen (A Norwegian Woman Using the Telephone)	Ethel Olson
	En Norsk Dame ved Strandbreden (A Norwegian Woman at the Beach)	Ethel Olson
72077	Mot Kveld (Eventide)	Eleonora Olson
	Syng kun i din ungdoms vaar (Youth's Song in Springtime)	Ethel & Eleonora
72183	Sogne Kjaering—Forste Part (The Old Woman from Sogn)	Eleonora Olson
	Sogne Kjaering—Anden Part (The Old Woman from Sogn)	Eleonora Olson
72323	Bliv hos mig, Mester (Abide With Me)	Ethel & Eleonora
	O Herre (Oh Lord)	Eleonora Olson
72412	Bissam, bissam baadne (Rock-a-bye) (2) Killebukken, lammet mit (The Lambkin)	Eleonora Olson
	Byssan lu, byssan lei (Lullaby)	Eleonora Olson
72657	Det nye Piano (The New Piano)	Ethel Olson
	Piano lektionen (The Piano Lesson)	Ethel Olson
72930	Det nye bokskap (The New Book-Case)	Ethel Olson
	Den leende pike hos fotografen (The Laughing Girl at the Photographer's)	Ethel Olson
73086	Naa de brente hos Kniperuds (The Fire at Kniperud's)	Eleonora Olson
	I kveld er eg glad (I Am So Happy To-night)	Eleonora Olson
77286	Trial Marriage	Eleonora Olson
	A Delicatessen	Ethel Olson
77517	Kvindeforeningen (The Ladies Aid)	Eleonora Olsen
	Kaffeslabberas (Over the Coffee Cups)	Eleonora Olsen
77251	Paa kinomatografen (At the Movies)	Ethel Olson
	Basebalspillet (The Baseball Game)	Ethel Olson

Form No 7296 ia October 1924 Norwegian English

INTRODUCTION

Between 1905 and 1925 Eleonora and Ethel Olson were well-known figures in Scandinavian communities throughout the United States. They toured extensively in the Midwest, and their recordings on the Victor and Brunswick labels gained them a nationwide following.

The sisters were versatile performers, adept at both singing and comedy. They usually worked with a piano accompanist and presented a program of vocal works, piano solos, and comic monologues. Eleonora, a contralto, was the primary vocalist, and Ethel, a soprano, joined her for duets. Their musical repertoire ranged from opera arias and art songs to familiar old Norwegian songs and American standards. They were well-dressed women, on stage and off, but in her readings Eleonora took on the guise of a Norwegian peasant by covering herself with a shawl.

Ironically, the Olson Sisters' fame rested less on their serious musical ability than on their original Norwegian dialect stories. "Isn't it funny vit people here in America," says the woman in **Veddingen Til Mabel**, "dey don't talk Norvegian and dey don't talk English."

Eleonora and Ethel, whose parents were from Norway, portrayed the immigrant's difficulty in adapting to American life. Their story **At The Movies** touches on homesickness for the Old Country while **The Baseball Game** recounts a Norwegian woman's misadventures with the national pastime. The humor in the stories rings true because the Olson Sisters knew their subject firsthand — whether it be a meeting of the ladies' aid, a piano lesson, or a scene witnessed on a train. In **The Old Sogning Woman** Eleonora used the dialect of her mother's birthplace.

A magazine article from 1924 relates how Ethel drew upon an incident in real life for her sketch **A Norwegian**

Woman At The Telephone: "One day as a little girl Ethel visited an ice cream parlor. While there her attention was attracted to a woman who had been called to the telephone for the first time in her life. This experience occasioned considerable fright, and a very humorous conversation ensued. A couple of weeks later Ethel was performing before a large gathering in Orchestra Hall, Chicago; being called upon for an encore, she gave the story."

The same article says of Eleonora: "It is somewhat surprising that Eleonora Olson, who speaks so many different dialects of Norway, was born in Chicago and has never been abroad. Norwegians say that her enunciation and articulation are just the same as a native's." (A sample of her dialect skill can be heard on the comic recordings she did in Norwegian: **Sogne Kjerring** and **Kaffeslabberas**.)

During their peak touring years the Olson Sisters, who then lived in Chicago, had a home away from home at Mrs. Dikka Koren's boarding house in Minneapolis. Other notable Norwegian-Americans also stayed there such as J.A.O. Preus who was a future governor of Minnesota and the painter Herbjørn Gausta. Agnes Preus, Mrs. Koren's niece, recalls that the boarders were a convivial group: "At the dinner table there were stories all the time. I can remember it was hard to eat a meal because we spent so much time laughing." One of the boarders was a young musician named A. C. Askegaard. He later married Virginia Bing, a niece of Eleonora and Ethel.

While on tour the Olson Sisters appeared in small town opera houses, civic halls, churches, and college auditoriums. In the summer, when warm weather made these facilities unusable, they performed in the big brown tents of the traveling Chautauqua.* Eleonora and Ethel were perennial favorites with the Chautauqua's rural audiences; in 1915, for instance, they were booked for the entire summer season on the circuit.

An article from that same year in *Sanger-Hilsen* comments on their popularity: "Among the many troupes that visit us out here in the West, Eleonora Olson's takes a leading place. While the others cease operation after one or two seasons, these three ladies return invariably year after year, and one new city after the other is added to their tour. And this is as it should be; for they bring with them much cheerfulness." The article praises the musical talent of the sisters and their accompanist, and of Ethel it says: "Her Norwegian dialect stories can make even the most stiff-necked pessimist curl up with laughter."

Eleonora and Ethel came from a musical family. Their brother, Jacob Alexander Bing, sang for many years with light opera companies. Their mother, Johanna, also had a fine singing voice, and the *Minneapolis Daglig Tidende* credited her with having instilled a love of music in her children. A witty and charming person, Johanna undoubtedly contributed to her daughters' sense of humor as well.

Eleonora was much older than Ethel and performed for several years before teaming up with her in 1909. Although she had been a child prodigy, Eleonora did not become a full-time professional singer until in her thirties. She attended Chicago Musical College for two years, but a lack of funds prevented her from continuing her musical training. A 1902 article in the St. Paul newspaper *Nordvesten* says this about Eleonora: "That she can sing what she sings, in the manner which she does, with only those opportunities she has had, is the best proof of her more than usual gifts . . . Until now she has unfortunately had to give up the thought of devoting herself completely to her art . . . She herself says that she has had to struggle for everything she has become."

In 1905 Eleonora joined the Skovgaard Concert Company, and for the next twenty years she actively pursued a musical career. She was frequently a guest soloist with choirs, glee clubs, and choruses and sang both sacred and secular music.

Ethel too showed early promise and started her career as a reader (actress) at the age of five. She was an accomplished pianist and won a number of musical scholarships. As an adult, however, her greatest acclaim was as a comedienne.

The Olson Sisters knew many important people. Among their friends were U.S. Senator Henrik Shipstead and his wife and such leading families of the church as the Preuses, the Stubs, and the Korens. After a performance on the road, Eleonora and Ethel were often the overnight guests of prominent local citizens.

By the early 1920's Eleonora, Ethel, and their mother all resided in Minneapolis. Eleonora and Johanna, who shared an apartment, were members of Our Saviour's Lutheran Church. Ethel and her husband attended Central Lutheran Church.

When Ethel married Dr. R. M. Pederson in 1923, the Olson Sisters stopped touring. They still made records, though, and in 1925 published a collection of their humorous stories called *Yust For Fun*.

In recent years stories from the book have been performed at the Nordic Fest in Decorah, Iowa and at the Snoose Boulevard Festival in Minneapolis. *Yust For Fun* has long been out of print. Eggs Press is now re-publishing it so that modern readers can enjoy this comic masterpiece.

*Suggested reading on the Chautauqua movement and rural entertainment in the early 1900's:

Morrison, Theodore. *Chautauqua.* Chicago: The University of Chicago Press, 1974.

Slout, William Lawrence. *Theatre In A Tent.* Bowling Green, Ohio: The Bowling Green University Popular Press, 1972.

NOTES

Photographs and background material for this edition of *Yust For Fun* were furnished by Mr. & Mrs. Paul R. Askegaard. Paul's mother, Virginia, is the Olson Sisters' niece.

The drawings on pages 22, 34, and 40 are by Paul's daughter, Ruth Askegaard. The unsigned drawings on pages 13 and 25 were in the earlier editions of the book. There is a good possibility that these were drawn by the Olson Sisters' friend, Herbjørn Gausta.

Other sources of information were the Norwegian-American Historical Association, the Olle i Skratthult Project, and George T. Springer.

This edition of the book differs from the earlier ones in that two stories have been added and one omitted. The added stories are **The Baseball Game** and **A Norwegian Woman At The Beach**. They were transcribed from 78 rpm recordings. The story omitted was **Sogne Kjerring**, a Norwegian language version of **The Old Sogning Woman**.

The setting of **The Baseball Game** is Chicago. These Minneapolis locations are mentioned elsewhere in the book: Minnehaha Falls, Milwaukee Avenue, Cedar Avenue, and Seven Corners.

Minnehaha Falls is the scene every summer of large gatherings of Scandinavians when on three different Sundays in June and July the Danes, Swedes, and Norwegians celebrate their heritage with religious services, speeches, entertainment, and traditional foods. Milwaukee Avenue is a short, narrow street which was once largely inhabited by immigrant railroad workers. In the 1970's the street has been closed to traffic, and many of its Victorian style homes have been renovated. Cedar Avenue and Seven Corners are in the heart of what was formerly a Scandinavian neighborhood. The Olson Sisters performed at nearby Dania Hall, which has been designated a historical landmark building. The Snoose Boulevard Festival was held in the area from 1972 to 1977.

The word **de** is used in dialect to represent the English words **the** and **they** and the Norwegian word **det** (it). **Ve** and **vi** are both used to mean the English **we**.

CONTENTS

PREFACE

DURING our many concert tours thru the great Northwest we have had numerous requests for our own original Norwegian dialect stories, so we have decided to give them to the public in the form of this book, and hope they will succeed in making you laugh.

We wish to emphasize that these monologues are not intended to ridicule our beloved country people but are given as typical character studies.

We find that the Scandinavians themselves are the first to enter into the hearty enjoyment of these stories.

YUST *for* FUN

THE OLD SOGNING WOMAN

I DON'T suppose der is very many here dat remembers me ven I vas young. Den I vas de center of attraction ver ever I vent – de boys yusto stand around as tick as flies on a yug of molasses, and I could have had every von of dem, but I could never make up my mind; I vas a regaler budderfly—but I flied around too long, and ven I should look around and tink about to get married, dere vasn't von single von left, but dat old Tutle-brok dat I took. But I tot it vas better den notting *(I vouldn't be old maid for anyting, I tot, dat time)* and so ve got splisa up.

Men I hasn't been happy von single day since dat time, I didn't have so much as a cellar—dat hole he called cellar vas so full of vater, dat if I yust lift up de luka, den de rats and de toads and de frogs and de snakes vould yump out on de floor. So I had to keep de milk and de eggs and de butter standing under de bed.

And dat old lobster he didn't do notting but talk about running. He run in de spring and he run in de fall. So I said to him von night after ve vent to bed: "If you is so crazy to run, vy don't you run after de cows and de pigs, because de is over in de neighbors field all de time."

But den I tell you he got mad, oh goodness me, how mad he got—he laid and scolded de whole night long, so I couldn't sleep a vink—I yust rolled and cried and tot how different tings could have been, if I had looked out in time. And de first ting I know, dere vas an awful crash and de bed, she broke right in two, and I fell right down in all dat good milk and cream and ven I should look, Pa vas sitting up in a yar of butter—but I got up so qvick som I could and started to dip up de cream and I vas so partiklar and took so nice of de top and put up in de churn. But I guess der vas still many tings der dat shouldn't be, because ven I come into town, de storekeeper, he said: "Vill you please bring de butter in by heself and de rusk and de bugs by sheself? and I can mix dem ven I get dem here."

I got mad den, and said: "I don't tink you got anybody som bring better budder den me, and I came in today because I vant to get me a bottle me Pinkham."

But I didn't get as much as a few drops of peppermint on a piece of sugar from him—I had to go limping home vit my butter.

I didn't understand vat Pa vas running after, you see, but it vas someting in de polltiks—I don't know if it vas road-boss or guvnor or yanitor, or vus it sinator; goodness knows he vas sint enough or mad, some you call it; maybe it vas *mad*-jistrate.

Vell, den he vanted to move into town, because he tot he

could get anyting in de pollticks, if he yust come to town. Oh my, I never forget de day before ve moved into town, de chickens and de gooses and de turkies vent over in de corner and cackled, it sounded yust exactly like a ladies' aid society—dey seemed to understand dat I vas going; and de first ting I knew dey came valking around, you know, and laid dere eggs right in front of me—and dey got so execisa dey vent around tree-four times—I didn't have more den ten chickens, but I got tirty til forty eggs dat day.

And de cows and de calfs, dey stood looking on vit de tears yust trilling down dere cheeks and I cried and felt so bad dat de neighbors had to yust come and lead me avay. I never lived any odder place but de farm, and vot vas I going to do in town, ver I couldn't have so much som a cat of my own. Aa ja, aa ja, aa du, aa du!

Vell, den ve moved into town—into a good for notting old shack, ver de vind blowed in from von corner and out de next. Men den I tell you I got sick; oh yiminy Christmus, how sick I got. I got amonia on der lungs, den I got brown kittens, I got so brown in de face and ven I vould draw my bret, it sounding yust like I had de whole neck full of kittens. Den I tink it vas around Pintse time or Penticast, you know, den I got pintsecise or pentacise or vat ever you call it. And den I got romantismus. Pa he vas so awful to snore, so I couldn't lay in de house, so I vent out in de barn and sleep in de hayloft and I know it's from dat I got dat awful hayfeber.

But it made no døffense how sick I vas, he had to have pie every day, of kors I et it too sometimes, and den I got dis awful pie-rea in de teet; Pa vas alvays yellous of my teet because de vas exactly like pearls—but now, I suppose I got to pull everyvon of dem out.

And dat old vind-bag didn't get any yob in de pollatick

atall. He yust vent over on de depot and look on de train come in and gab vit de men and look at de girls. And he got so dirty over on de depot, dat I have to stand at home in de vashtub and vash out his old dirty overalls and shirts—and from standing so much in de tub, I got tubicolosis.

Oh, gooness me, how sick I vas—. And everybody said I should go to doktor—but dere vasn't anyting but a good-for-notting Yankee doktor in town; and dey don't understand anyting about Norvegian sickness—because ven I told him how sick I vas, he said: "You got Maggienation." "Oh, for goodness sake," I said, "has I got dat sickness, too? I suppose you is going to operate on me den," and he said: "Oh, forget it, old girl, take a valk out in de sunshine and cut out de coffee and you vill be awright." And I said: "You can cut out anyting you vant to, but please don't cut out de coffee, because dat is all dat holds life in me."

But I could learn dot doktor a ting or two about sickness—didn't I had all dose books from Pinkham and Kuriko? and de vas von time in de spring, I had eighty-tree sicknesses in de Kuriko book, and von hundred and tventy-tree in de Pinkham book.

But you should see how full of pep de old man is getting now. He is standing out in de kitsen and pressing out his pants and putting on a necktie and collar and starting to show off vørs den ever. He tinks I am going to lay down and die and he is going to get dose pennies I have been scraping togedder—*but I ain't dead yet!*

A BUSY PIANO TEACHER

VELL, do you tink you know any more about piano playing dis veek den you did last veek? I suppose you understand dat piano playing isn't all monkey-bisness. No siree, it takes real vork to play de piano.

Say, you better take dose rubbers on de outside. You can't come in de house vit such dirty rubbers. And look at your fingers; my, men de is dirty. Did you stop and play marbles on de vay to your piano teacher's house? I vant to ask you vun qvestion—do you tink dat Rachmaninoff or Paderewski or Hoffman or Bauer, vould stop and play marbles on de vay to dere piano teacher's house? No, you bet dey vouldn't. Dey vould valk right straight to de teacher's house.

Now sit down on de benk and sit up straight like a "soldat" and don't put your feet on de *pedals.* First ve play vit de fingers and aftervhile vit de *pedals.* Now ve vill play dat five finger exercise and count four for each note and count out loud, because dat is de main ting. Vun, two, tree, four, vun, two, tree four; say, vat is de matter vit you? I can't hear you counting. Can't you count out loud? And vhy do you hold your fingers dat vay? Vhy do you hold dem so much like a pitchfork? Vhy don't you bend dem over a little bit, so dey look more like a rake? Start over again. Vun, two, tree, four; say, you ain't tinking about vat you are doing atall. You better play dat piece you have been playing for de last six munce and see if you can't do dat better.

(Counts and sings, keeping time with the music, teaches and keeps up conservation with friend, in singing voice.)

Vun, two—vun, two—*How do you do—how are you today?—sit right down—I'll be tru—puddy soon*—Vun, two—*My you are looking—awful good today*—vun, two:

(To the pupil): Because I am talking to de lady, do you have to stop in your piano playing?—your business is to play. Start over again. Vun, two—vun two—*Vere did you get—dat puddy dress—you got on?*—Vun, two—vun, two,—*Did you have a dressmaker*—vun, two,—*did she use a pattern—or cut it out of her head*—Vun, two—vun, two—*dat panel in de back—looks awful good on you*—vun, two—Say vat is de matter vit you? You don't tink about vat you are doing atall. I vant to ask you a qvestion—vat is de first ting you got to learn in piano playing? Vat did you say? De first ting you got to do is to learn to play "yazz"?—I vill certainly yazz you. Vot you got to learn to do, is to *concentrate.* You take dat lesson home and see if you can't do better next time.

VEDDINGEN TIL MABEL

MABEL'S WEDDING

OH, Miss Snurpe, I'm so glad I got hold on you, I tot I should never found you. I called up Mrs. Larson because I know you used to vent dere so much and I said, could you tell me vere I could find Miss Snurpe? And do you know, she said somting awful funny, she said: "Miss Snurpe, don't come here no more because my brudder are married now." Vasn't dat a funny ting to say? Den she suyyested I should call up Mrs. Yohnson (you know coalman Yohnson). And I called up Mrs. Yohnson and dat's de vorst ting I ever did; I got dat old man Yohnson on de telephone and I couldn't unnerstan a vord he said.

He said you vas living on Minnehaha Falls—de kunne jeg forstaa—but he said, "If you take de street car you'll never find it, and if you go to de falls you're lost."

Isn't it funny vit people here in America, dey don't talk Norvegian and dey don't talk English.

So I called up Mrs. Hickson *(she is Yankee)* and I could good unnerstan her. She said: "Miss Snurpe var here and sewed for me, but she are gone and she don't left no telephone number, but I tink I can told you how to found her. You valk up Cedar Avne till you come to Seven Corner, den you snu to de left and dere's a big red house on de corner, but it ain't dat vun; den it's two more, but it ain't dose, but it's de house next to de two vat it ain't; it are standing kind of far back on de lot."

So I took my girl Myrtle (she is crazy to ride on de street car) and ve found de place alright, and de lady vas awful nice; she said: "I'm sorry, Miss Snurpe are gone on her vacation and I don't know ven she come back." Oh, I vas so dissapointa, I yust come home and cried. And Papa said: "Mama, vy are you crying?" I said: "Here Mabel are going to get married and I ain't got no dress to put on, and Miss Snurpe have gone on her vacation." And Papa said: "Cut out dat sob stuff, Mama, and ve vil go on a good movie," and ve vent.

I never go on movie, men dis vas a good vun. Ve vent and seed, I tink it vas "De four horseback riders (Four Horsemen) of de poker chips." My, men dat vas good, I never enyoy anyting so much; I cried tru de hole ting. Oh, it vas yust grand.

Ven ve came out in front, I vanted to look at de pitchers of de actoreens, and who should stand right in front of me but your yentleman frand. I vas yust ready to hug him. I said: "Could you tell me vere I could find Miss Snurpe?"

And he looked so glad and said: "Yes, o'kors, she is living on de Young Vomen's Christian Assassination."

Oh, Miss Snurpe, I'm so glad you could come and yelp, but betveen mig aa dig, Miss Snurpe, I ain't so glad in dis vedding som I skud be. Ven I tink of all de fellers Mabel could of had. Dey vas yust crazy for her and dey all had grand automobiles. You remember Mr. Vilbur from Vilmet, don't you? he had fifty tousand in his own ret. He was yust crazy for Mabel, he vould come here and call me "mama" and give me candy; oh, he vas so sveet and he had a grand Fierce-Sparrow car—dats vun of de best cars you can get. But do you tink Mabel vanted him? No, he vus too tin on de top.

And den dat preacher; he came from von of de finest families you can come from—dey vas preachers vay back to de time of Moses. He called me "mama" too, and he had a nice "Dirt" car. I don't know if de vas Dirt or Dort, but de vas someting like dat. But do you tink Mabel vanted him? oh, no, he vas too slow.

And den dat grand banker dat vas crazy for Mabel. He vas in everyting grand. He vas a Elk's tooth, he vas a Skriner, he belonged to de Sons of Norvay, I tink he even belonged to de Daughters of Norvay. And he had de svellest Kakelak car or vas it Cadillac, vell it vas vun of dose real grand vuns. He vould stand outside and honk and honk for Mabel, but she didn't care for him; because he vas too fat.

And now she's crazy for Clarence and all he's got is a second-handy Ford. And yust tink, she could have had a "Kakelak."

Vell, I can't tink about dat now, I got to get someting to vear. Say, vat can you do vit dis dress, Miss Snurpe? You see I have had it since Mabel vas confirmera; you know it's a little vide in de shirt, couldn't you draping it up on de side and cut off de arms and ring out de neck, and fix de up so good som you can?

Ven I tink of it, she's only getting a Ford—and she says I vould radder have Clarence vit his Ford den all de fellers I know.

Now dey are practicing de vedding march (Lohengrin's march), tra-la-la-la, tra-la-la-la-la; don't you hear dem?

My, he's good to look at and he's young, and he ain't so bowlegged, and Mabel says: "Ma, you shouldn't vorry, he's going to be a civilized enyineer," so maybe it von't be so bad.

Vell, hurry up Miss Snurpe, and do de best you can, I can't stand around here all day, I got to go and make lefse and fløtegrøt for de vedding. Men I say, if Mabel had taken vun of dose odder beaux I vould have got a fine gray silk dress.

THE TRIAL MARRIAGE

OF kors you heard dat Betsy left Ole? Oh yes, I suppose dey vas as happy as de rest of us. But de vimen iss different from ven ve vas young. You can't vipe your feet on dem, saa dei gjore me oss, naar vi va onge.

You remember vat a dude Ole vas, he had to have everyting better den de rest of de boys, even his overalls vas fancier and no girl vas good enough for him til he met Betsy. But den he got bissy; my goodness how he vaited on her. He took her buggy riding and he'd bring a pint of ice cream almost every time he called on her. He seemed to tink it vas a great honor to take her out, and it vas. Betsy vas fine

"Ole sat yust like he vas hypnotisa."

looking, had a good figger and valked exactly like a qveen, and smart—she could have been a schoolteacher or a typewriter or anyting she vanted to be if she had had a chance to finish her edication.

Dei sa da, at han va so nervous, naar han proposa, at ho kunde mest intje høira maule pau han.

Of kors he carried on de vay all of dem do, and asked if she vould take him for life. But you see, Betsy knew how his fader treated his moder; it vas as if she vas an old rocking chair—good enough ven he vas tired, but in de vay de rest of de time.

So Betsy told him, "No, Ole, I can't promise more den five years, but if ve are satisfied at de end of dat time, ve can renew de lease." And he vas so happy he looked silly.

Betsy made von mistake; she vated too much on him.

An Betsy iss an awful good cook and very eekonimical. But it vasn't many days before he commenced to kick because she used too much milk and cream. And dere she had a fine cow she brought vit her from home; vun of dose fine milkers, she vas a padegreed cow—took premi pau kounty fair. But Ole alvays gave Betsy's cow de poorest hay and if he vas cross about anyting he vould kick Betsy's cow; and dat hurt Besty, you know how awful tender hearted she iss.

But Betsy vas alvays nice and pleasant. In de evening Ole vould talk polletick to de hired man or play solitary, and Betsy vould read or sew.

About two veeks ago Betsy fixed up in some of her best and had a flower in her hair and made a grander supper dan usual and she vas standing in de door vaiting for Ole. Ven he came, he took de vash dish and dipped in de rain barrel and vashed and splashed.

Ven he vas viping his face he said: "Vat are you all upholstered for?"

She said: "Don't you know vat day dis iss?"
"Sure," he said, "it's Saturday, ain't it?"
"Yes," she said, "it's de sevent of Yune."
"Vell, vat of it," he said.
"It's our vedding day," Betsy said.
"Sevent of Yune," he said, "by golly, dat's de day dey got dat auction over to de Larson farm, I got to hurry up and go."

Betsy never said a vord til supper vas over, den she said: "You better look for a housekeeper at de same time vhile you is over to Larson's."

He said: "Vhat's de matter vit you?"

"Notting," she said, "but de five years is up, you haven't lived up to your end of de deal and I'm tru."

Vell, de hired man said he sat yust like he vas hypnotisa for hours, he forgot all about de auction and everyting else, and ven he came to his senses, Betsy vas gone.

And Ole is de saddest looking dude you ever saw. Betsy von't see him, so he goes and plays sveet on her moder. He has bought a automobile and has promised her a new house and a vashing-machine and dat she can use all de money from de eggs and chickens for herself, if she vil only come back to him. Aa, ja, men sa eg smør, he's trying to bribe her.

Vel, I alvays said Betsy isent any fool.

ELEONORA OLSON CONCERT TRIO

For terms address,

ELEONORA OLSON CONCERT TRIO,

2148 N. Sawyer Ave., Chicago, Ill. 1708 Elliot Ave., Minneapolis, Minn.

Comments of the Press

At Studebaker Hall

ELEONORA OLSON sang with deep, powerful voice in a manner most artistic. She possesses a most charming stage appearance and manner, which added to a rich mezzo soprano voice captivated her audience.

—Chicago Tribune.

MISS ELEONORA OLSON
MEZZO SOPRANO

St. Paul Pioneer Press.

Eleonora Olson has a sympathic contralo voice with a full volume of wide range. All her numbers were sung with thoughtful interpretation, but none were more effectiveley given than her last group, especially "Forgetfulness," by Hildach.

Minneapolis Times.

Eleonora Olson's singing was the most artistic on the program, and her voice seemed perfectly adequate to fill every corner of the Auditorium. She sings with a marked sympathy and constantly betrays the temperament of the musician. Her voice seemed last night to possess great carrying power, for even her softest pianissimo could be heard in extreme back of the hall.

St. Pauls Dispatch.

A warm welcome was offered the contralto, Miss Eleonora Olson, whose full and even scale, warm and luscious tones and artistic ideals made her contributions to the program unqualified pleasures. She sang "My Heart at thy Sweet Voice," from "Samson and Deliah," with fine phrasing and expression, and in Becker's "Fruehlingszeit," revealed herself an artist of sufficient temperament and grace. Two Norwegian songs were sung in excellent style, and in Roma's "Separation," for which Mr Skovgard played an obligatio, there was a remarkable sympathy between the tone of the Stradivarius and that of the 'cello-like contralo. Miss Olson made, indeed a pleasing impression, her appeal being quite broad enough to include the cultivated palate and popular taste.

Decorah Republican.

Since her last appearance in Decorah, Miss Eleonora Olson has developed both vocally and artistically, and she brought back to her friends strength, sweetness and purity of voice such as she gave promise of possessing in her earlier concert in Decorah. It was a delight to hear her again.

a

b

c

d

e

f

g

h i

j k

l m

ELEONORA OLSON

AND

ETHEL OLSON

IN

SONGS AND READINGS

Programme

ELEONORA OLSON
MEZZO SOPRANO

ETHEL OLSON
SOPRANO AND READER

ASSISTED BY
ROSETTA OLSON, PIANIST

1. **Capriccio** - - - - - - - - *Mendelssohn*
   Rosetta C. Olson
2. **Aria from Samson and Delila** - - *Saint Saens*
   Eleonora Olson
3. **The District School** - - - -
   Ethel Olson
4. (*a*) **O, Herre** - - - - - - *Melartin*
   (*b*) **Mot Kveld** - - - - - *Grondahl*
   (*c*) **Lille Grete** - - - - - - *Gade*
   Eleonora Olson
5. **Morning** - - - - - - - - *Grieg*
   Rosetta C. Olson
6. **A Rural Song** - - - - - *Dell Acqua*
   Ethel Olson
7. **At a Glove Counter** - - - - -
   Ethel Olson
8. (*a*) **Florian's Song** - - - - - - *Godard*
   (*b*) **Little One a Crying** - - - - *Speak*
   (*c*) **Separation** - - - - - - *Roma*
   Eleonora Olson
9. (*a*) **That Old Sweetheart of Mine** - - *Riley*
   (*b*) **Home, Sweet Home** - - - - -
   Ethel Olson
10. **The Passage Bird's Farewell** - - - *Hildach*
    Eleonora and Ethel Olson

MISS ALICE R. WALDEN
PIANISTE

Miss Walden at Edgerton, Wis.

Miss Alice I. Walden, the pianiste, was especially well appreciated. Each of her numbers were enthusiastically received and were well deserving of the encore which they received. Miss Walden's two best numbers were probable "Carnival of Venice," by Schulhoff, and "Polka de la Reine," of Raff. They were played as were all of her selections, with ease and delicacy of touch. Her tone was beautiful and her technique equals that of any pianist that has ever been here. She held her audience at closest marked attention and during the playing of the light, soft passages a pin might have been heard dropping, so wonderfully dainty aud easy were they executed. As an accompanist Miss Walden here, too, displayed her great ability, and played with refined style in all her accompanying. Too much could not possibly be said of Miss Walden's playing and every one who heard her says she is truly a great artist.

Crookston, Minn., Daily Times

Miss Alice R. Walden, who played a number of piano solos, shared in more than equal measure the approval given the other artists. Her techi nique blended with the sympathetic interpretation given the master pieces. She left no doubt as to her ability, and her graceful manner of responding to the insistance of the audience was pleasing.

Omaha World

Miss Walden has astounding power and wields it with an ease that is bewildering, and she also has an exquisite daintiness and delicacy of touch.

Valley City, N. D., Times Herald

The concert given by the Eleonora Olson Concert Trio as the Armory was a decided success and by many pronounced to be one of the best of the season. Miss Walden is a pianist whose playing is marked by a smooth technique and refined taste, and she compares favorably with such as artist as Miss Showers, who assisted Madame Nordica at her concert at the Auditorium not long ago. Miss Walden gave a splendid rendition of Greig's "Wedding Day" and Listz's Hungarian Rhapsody, "The Trout," by Schubert-Heller, and "Polka de la Reine" by Raff, all of which she played with true musical temperament and artistic finish, to which added not least her admiringly skillful use of the pedal. It is to be hoped that this splendid concert trio can be heard once more in Valley City this season and by larger audience than before.

Miss Walden in Chicago

Paa programmet var tre pianonumre of henholdsvis Rubenstein, Chop og Grieg, og under stod novnet: Alice Rossing Walden. Man forstod disse skulde være Aftenens Glansnumra of haabede de ogsaa vilde bli Ingen blev skuffet. Den tækkelige unge, sortklædte dame, som sa til Flygelet viste sig at være i besiddelse af baade hol teknik og mindelig musikalsk smag. Hun gav det meste personlige udtr russiske Romance som hun spillede rent ud sagt deiligt. Skan

Ethel C. Olson in Eau Claire

MISS ETHEL C. OLSON
SOPRANO AND IMPERSONATOR

MISS ETHEL OLSON followed in her clever and wonderful impersonation. No mere words can do justice to this charming and talented lady and the pen can only exhaust itself in superlatives. Miss Olson is an artist in her line of work. She is the most clever and remarkable impersonator that ever appeared before an Eau Claire audience. She made a tremendous hit. Encore followed encore. She possesses a rich dramatic voice and a charming personality.

North-west Review.

Of the six contestants in the annual declamation contest Miss Ethel C. Olsen easily ranked first; her rendition of Hagar was excellent. She posseses a rich, dramatic voice and also a charming personality. She immediately captivated the audience as well as the judges, who awarded her first prize.

Skandinaven.

Miss Ethel Olson is an elocutionist of remarkable power, and to her art she unites not only a graceful figure, but a charmingly expressive face, The selections were well chosen and received unstinted applause from the audience, which demanded several encores.

The Willmar Gazette.

Miss Ethel was by far the cleverest reader that has been heard in Willmar for many moons. She had the knack of getting right to her audience's funny spot and after her first appearance, everybody laughed the minute she came in view. She was irresistible. Fun peeked out of her eyes and was radiated everywhere melting the most unhappy countenance in the hall into lingering smiles.

"From Long Ago to Now," was one of her best numbers, but "the" effo t of the evening was her owny own, that means original, "Norwegian Woman Using the Telephone for the First Time," reading which was entertainingly ridiculous. "The Newly-weds First Quarrel" was another number that she gave towards the end of the program that raised the already high spirit of mirth of the audience up a notch higher. Miss Olson can sing as well as read and she has a fascinating soprano voice.

Forest City, Iowa

The reading selections of Miss Ethel Olson were all of the humorous ain and her rendition was of that natural, easy-going, off-hand way that npels one not only to hear but feel the fullness of the subject being dled.

Chicago Daily News, at Orchestra Hall

Miss Ethel Olson simply brought down the house in her character nations. Encore followed upon encore, and the audience refused t in its applauding. Her impersonation made a tremendous hit. son also has a most beautiful soprano voice.

THE FIRE AT KNIPERUD'S

I HASN'T been feeling good for a long time, men I tink de come from de fire dey had over to Kniperud's. Hasn't you heard of de? My, de vas awful.

You know Mrs. Kniperud, she don't care to bodder over houseverk or anyting like dat, she yust like to play britch (you know vat I mean, cards), dessa stygge, du vet; dat's someting I never do. Den she like to go to movie show and such tings. Men ven she going to have a svell party, den she alvays get me to bake for her. Vell, if I has to say de myself, I don't tink dere's anyvun can beat me to bake. I can bake cookies—eight kind of cookies and fattigman and lefse and kromkaker, berline-kranser and fry kake, aa anyting you vant, if I yust get someting to bake off. Men de trouble are, dey vant me to use saapestut for butter, saapestut for eggs and everyting. Dey begin dat de time ve has dat var (war). Men it seems like ven I bake, de taste good anyvay.

Vell, I vas going to tell about de fire. Mrs. Kniperud vas going to St. Apolis to handle Christmas presents, and Earl, her boy, should stay at home and help me. Ja, de va fin hjærp. He eat up de cookies and de fry kake so qvick som I can make dem and of kors I didn't have any vood to put in de stove, so I said to Earl: "Earl," sa jeg, "von't you plees go out and hug me a armful of vood. You can't blame your papa if he don't hug, he get tired snikkering around de church." *(Du veit han snikkrer paa denna nye matodist kjerka).* He building on dat new church.

Men, you know Earl he are fresh, som dey say, he got answer for everyting. *(De a slik kjeft paa'n)*, he say, you don't know my pa, he iss never too tired to hug my ma. I said you should shame yourself, Earl, to talk like diss; go out and get de vood. Den he could see I vas mad, so he vent out and came in vit a big armful of vood. Men jeg synes, de lugta gasoline, so I say, Earl, dat vood smells gasoline, and he say, you is krasy; dat's perfume I got from my girl.

I put de vood in de stove, and my goodness, dere vas a awful explosen and everyting fly off de stove and de fire spruta out all over and de shimney get all red, and I run fort and back and didn't know vat to do. I never use de phome in my life, so I tell Earl to phome his papa; I said tell him dere is fire in de shimney. But he yust scream and laugh and said, "Oh, you vant to dance de shimmey? Or right, I put some 'yazz' on de phonegraph den."

Men den de fire vas coming out of de roof and everyting and I run and talked in the phome myself and I yell, hurry up, fire apartment, deres fire in Kniperud's pipe. Men dey yust laugh on me in de telephone. Men I vas yust out of my shær me skrek, and I yust skreem Hang me on de line me Kniperud, de's fire in de shimney, dat dey could unnerstan. Den pudy soon de fire-apartment come and skvirt vater and de cookies and de fry kake vas yust von puddle. Men dem seva meste ta huse. It vas Earl's room vat burnt de most and his new suit and everyting; men de var good enough for him.

You know he skul speaking on de Christmus tree de next day and didn't have notting to have on. Saa I say to Mrs. Kniperud, if you find a old suit of your husban', I tink I can make a suit for Earl.

Kors I didn't have any good pattern, saa maybe de don't fit som de skud, because ven my granson come home from de Christmus tree, he said, "Grandma, you should see how funny Earl Kniperud look ven he vas speaking on de Christmus tree, I couldn't tell if he vas coming or going, dere vas so funny shape on de pants."

It serve Earl right—he tink he are so much bedder den de rest.

Men de is værre for me, I got saa'n susing in de head all de time, after de fire so you must exchuse me, I can't hverken bake eller skrub today. Jeg filer saa funny.

(She is offered some coffee.) Aa, yes, tank you, maybe en draapa kaffe vould pep me up a little.

THE BOOKCASE

OH, I vas yust down on Milvaukee Avena (Avenue) and vas going to look after a bookcase for my man. You see, it's his birtday and I skul like to suprise him. Say, vat is de matter vit you children—can't you see mama is getting a suprise on papa?—You can't get up a suprise vit such kids around. But dat bookcase I saw on Milvaukee Avena, dat's de lovliest ting I ever saw. On de bottom of dis bookcase de vas two, vat you call it now, such um-um-um, such claws—vit de glass ball in de claws. It look yust like de vas a lion right in de room.

No, children, you can't have no sugar-lump, mama says no. Alright den, take it. And den you know, dis vas vat you call a combinason bookcase—if you feel like reading, you can read, and if you feel like writing, you can write—combinason, you understand. On de side vere you read dere vas vat you call a—now vat is de name of dat now—a bevla, ah um, oh, yes, beveled glass, and in dere you know you could have dishes and Skandinaven and Sears-Roebuck magazine and tings.

Vat is de matter vit you children—vell, take a bread slice, den—my goodness, dey is alvays bodering me vit someting. And den you know, on de side you write, dat vas good, dat ting you write on, ven dat vas up, dat vas ingrava vit bananas and peaches and grepes—you see dat vould look awful puddy in de dining room, too, you know. And you see, ven you let dat writing ting down, on de inside dere, it don't look like it should be anyting, men de var. De vas a secret drawer, you put your hand around de corner and press on someting, and de drawer come out and in dere my man could have his mortgages and bonds and gas bills and tings dat he's got, and money too, you know. Den ven he goes out, I go and look—don't de mans make you tired? Dey never vant you to know anyting about dere bisness.

Children, mama said no, you can't have no more sugar-lump. And den you know, up on top of de bookcase de vas a looking glass—de vas so high you couldn't look in it, men it vas awful puddy—it vas in de shape of a hjerte, you know in de shape of a heart. Vell, take a sugar-lump den and get out of here, mama is so shamed on you. And up on top of de looking glass de vas vat ve call in Norvegian, a dame-figur, you know a figger of a lady—you know vit a hat vit a fedder on de side and buttons down de front of de dress. If I could buy dat bookcase and suprise my hussban' I vould be de happiest voman in America, but I don' see how I'm going to get de money.

AT THE MOVIES

OH, my gooness, Mrs. Larson, men it's dark in here. Vy in de vorld do de have it so dark in de movie? Come on, Lily, hold on mama's shirt—I don't care if it's shirt or skirt, you take hold on it—you vant to fall down and break your neck, maybe, ha?

Come on, ve sit in here, Mrs. Larson, you sit down here. Come on, Lily, you sit next to mama—no you can't go down in front—you stay right here—after vhile it's going to be music and everyting. Vat you vant—ice cream cone—have you got nickle, den? Come here, boy, de little girl vants ice-cream cone, alright, give her Eskimo pie, den—now keep still for a vhile.

My, men I'm tired, Mrs. Larson. Ain't it crazy to run around like ve did and ve didn't get no bargains, ve could yust so good buy on Cedar Avenue, I tink. And such coffee—my, to pay five cents for such coffee, som ve had.

Vat's going on now? Oh, it's yust de ads. *(Reads ads.)* Vat's dat—boys' suits eight tirty-nine, oh, good night, tink to pay eight tirty-nine for a boy's suit. I made two pair of pants and a coat for Villie out of Pa's old suit, and it only cost me nickle for buttons. Oh my, dat's awful. *"Say it vit Flowers"*—dat dey can do after ve are dead; dey von't do it before.

Say, do you hear dat musik, Mrs. Larson? tra-la-la-la-la-la-la-la, do you know vot dat musik is? Dat's Norvegian musik. Listen, Lily, on dat musik, dey don't have dat kind of musik here—de's all "yazz" here. My gooness, Mrs. Larson, do you see vat's dere? *(Picture of Norway.)* Oh, to tink ve should come in here and see Norvay, *(cries softly)*. Oh, Lily, get up on de benk and look on Norvay. Isn't it lovely? to tink ve should come in here and see Norvay. Oh, I vish Papa vas here, he vould enyoy it so. See, looket de vay dey are fisking (fishing). Dat's Bergen, you know; dat's vere dey got de best fish. If ve could only get money saved up to go to Norvay on a trip; men dat ve never get. Now look, Lily, do you see dem yumping on skis? Oh my, men dat's fun. For de love of Mike, Mrs. Larson, look now. Do you see it? *Pepervika*—Lily, dat's vere Mama comes from—dat's de reason she's got so much pep. Oh my, men dis is good. To tink ve should come in here and see Pepervika; I forgot all about de pain in my foots.

Yes, Lily, here comes dat crazy-business you been vaiting for. Yes, dere he is, de silly ting. "Harold Lloyd in Safety Last." Ha-ha. He's good alright—ha-ha-ha. Oh my, looket, he are going to climb up de building. Oh my, he'll get killa.

Vhy do he do it? Now he are going to fall—oh no, he grabbed onto de clock. Oh, gooness, now he's starting up higher. How foolish he are. Oh gooness, oh my, grab onto someting; you vill kill yourself. O, poor ting, de policeman are after him. Oh, looket now—se paa'n (screams). De mouse are going up in his pants. Oh my, dat's de vorst. Oh, my, I'm so nervous, Mrs. Larson. Now, Lily, don't cry—de mouse von't come down here — de mouse are on de picture — dat's no vay for a big girl to act. See, look now, Lily, see he are up on de building and he vins de prize and gets his girl and everyting. Dat ain't notting to cry for.

Now ve got to go home. No, ve can't stay anodder minute. Mama's got to go home and make soup for Papa. You go first, Lily, go on—hurry up. Come on, Mrs. Larson. My, dat vas more fun dan I had for a long time. To tink I should see Pepervika.

THE LADIES' AID

President speaks:

LADIES, we will now discuss the surprise upon the preacher and his wife, whether we shall present them with a davenport or some aluminum ware. Mrs. Ole Jensen, what have you to say?

Mrs. Jensen speaks: Me and Mrs. Nelsen took a valk over to Olsen & Paulsen's furniture store last night and ve saw a awful puddy red sofa in de vindow, so I said to Mrs. Nelsen, let us go in and ask de price, and she said she tot ve shouldn't do dat, because she vould feel cheap to go out vitout buying it; but I said, I know Olsen so good. He used to come to our house so often ven vi lived on de farm, he used to sell trashing machines dat time. So ve vent in. And Olsen came up to vate on us, so I asked de price of de sofa, and Olsen said (I am almost ashamed to say vat he called de sofa), he said: "Dat Devil Port vil cost you $69.50." I said to him: "If dat is vat you call it, it is no use for us to look at it, because ve are looking for a present for de preacher and dat vil never do. He said: "Dere is notting wrong vit de name," he said, "sit down and try it." And ve did and it vas yust as if ve vas sitting in a fedder-bed. Vi sunk down so deep dat bote Olsen and Paulsen had to come and pull us out. De only trouble vit *dat* sofa is dat it is so comfortable dat de preacher's vife vill have company all de time—dey vill never vant to go home.

President: Thank you, Mrs. Jensen, it must have been a very nice davenport. What have you to say, Mrs. Rasmussen?

Mrs. Rasmussen *(Danish and very important and large):* Yes, I have seen dose Damingports, too; but de is not de latest. I have yust been down to Cicago to wisit my daughter—see has a very elegant home and see have vat vi calls in Danish, a Chisalonge—excuse me, I vill speak Inglish. In Inglish, I tink day calls it a Cheese longe. Only vone can sit in it at a time, and de usuly have a beautiful lamp in de back—and von can read or rest or do vat he like. —Den a maiet elegant.

President: What do you ladies think about buying the chaise-lounge?

Mrs. Monson *(thin and excited and energetic):* Yes, ve all seen plenty of dem Cheese-chairs—my daughter got von of dose, too. I don't give two cents for dem, only von can sit in it at de time, de takes up lots of room, den I tink it is much better to get von of dose ledder sofas dat you pulls out and can make up a bed for de extra company and gooness knows, de preacher have plenty of dat. But if you vant to know vat I tink—I tink ve should buy some alumni pans, because dat is someting dey vil need vorse den enyting else, because I know how it is ven I vas first married—I had only von pan, it vas sort of a milk pail and I cooked potatoes in it and I cooked kjøt-suppe in it, and I cooked coffee and everyting in it; so you see if somebody had got up a surprise on me and give me some luminee pans, I vould been tickla to death. And ve need so many tings in de church basement, right now ve need dish towels, ve need new coffee boiler, vi need some more cups. De coffee boiler leaked so de day ve entertained de Aiden fra vest side, at it ran alt over gørve. I vas so shamed I tot I vould never cook coffee any more. I tink de Devil Port are to expenser—men of kors vat ever you decide vil be alright for me.

President speaks: I see Grandma Bjelland wants to say something.

Grandma Bjelland *(a real commanding old lady from Stavanger):* I tink de førniture to de preacher is plenty good nuf. Vait to he have his tventy-five years fest, den you can buy all dis high-toned bisness. You talk so much about cheese lunch and Devil port—de vould be better if you talk about Himmel port—de er de værste eg ha hørt. And alummie pants; ve couldn't buy pants to fit de preacher—aa, intje vet vi seisen, ja kanskje eg ha blit old-fasoned, Kjøp kaa dok vil, men for goodness seke, kom me kaffen snart—eg e so kaffe tørst at eg kan mest intje svelje.

The hostess: Ja, vær saa god, kaffen er færdig.

(All the ladies rush for their refreshments—all talking at once.)

"And I slid."

THE BASEBALL GAME

OH, Mary, I'm glad you come because I got saa much to talking to you about. Do you know ver I vas yesterday, Mary? I bet you can't guess. I vas on a ballgame. Dat's de krasiest ting I ever vas to. I remember vun time ven before me and Ole vas married, you know—ve vas yust venting togedder—he asked me on de telephone if I vant to go and see de Tigers play de Cubs. I said sure, and I vent. And I vas vaiting all afternoon in front of de zoo at Lincoln Park, and Ole never come atall.

But yesterday Ole came home, and he vas all execisa. He said ve vas going on a baseball game and see de Vite Sox play. I vas on de downtown in de morning, and I bought a nice pair of dose cute little vite half-socks. Dere so nice and cool. Saa I tot if I vas going to a baseball game I vould put dem on.

My, men dere vas plenty people on dat ballgame. Goodness, saa mange folk har jeg aldri sett i mitt liv. Ve vas sitting dere real nice, and puddy soon, you know, dere vas an awful screaming. And I said, "Ole, vat's de matter now?" And vat do you tink he said, Mary—dat somevun had struck a fowl. Dat means a chicken, don't it. Yust tink, saa mean as to hit a poor little chicken.

And den dey started to yell and holler some more, and I said, "For de love of Mike, Ole, vat is it now?" And he said, somevun had caught a fly. Can you tink anyting saa dumb, Mary, *(laughing)* as to stop and catch a fly ven you're playing baseball. Oh, I tot it vas de krasiest ting.

But puddy soon Ole vas looking in de back of de grandstand, and he said a friend of his up dere had given him de high sign. I said, "Ole, vat do you mean by high sign?" He said, "I meant a high ball." Oh, I didn't know vat he meant, but den he vent up to see his friend, and he said, "You sit here and look on de game."

And I vas sitting dere, and saa I didn't enyoy it atall. But you know dat man dat has de stick, Mary, you know dat vun dat has de stick. He hit de ball awfully hard, and it yust flew over my vay. I turned around to look for Ole, and dere he vas up dere standing and yelling, "Come on home, you fool, come on home!" Vell, I vent up to him saa fast as I could, and ven I got up dere he yelled, "Go on back, you simp, go on back!" Oh, Mary, to tink dat Ole skud ever talk to me like dat. Oh, I felt saa bad.

I turned to go back, and yust den I slipped. And vould you believe it, Mary, dat Ole yelled, "Slide!" and every man in de grandstand vas yelling slide on me until dey vas purple in de face. And I slid until I come to a post.

Vell, puddy soon Ole come down to help me. Oh, I vas mad. I said, "Ole, vy are all dose men yelling on me?" Oh, he vas saa execisa. He said, "De Vite Sox has got a run in!" I says, "Vat do I care. I got anodder pair home, and you skud shame yourself to let all dose men yell on your vife."

LUK DOT VINDOW

WHILE on one of our many concert tours through the west, I saw quite a funny little scene and heard some humorous conversation. We were seated in a day coach when we were attracted by the voice of a tall gentleman of striking appearance, carrying a large violin case. It seems that he had been checking the baggage and the minute he came inside the door he talked loudly in Danish, "Nu har jeg checket baggashen, aa alting er i orden." He was in the rear of the coach and the ladies he was speaking to were seated up in front; the three were, apparently, a concert company. He came talking as he walked, and naturally everyone in the coach turned to see what was up. The coach was crowded and no seats to be had, so he said to the ladies: "You alvays get good seats, and here I must stand and hold dose heavy violins."

A gentleman directly opposite the ladies got up and offered him his seat, and the violinist was very happy and thanked him graciously. The first thing to arrest his attention was a family of five or six occupying a double seat in front of him, eating a most appetizing lunch of fried chicken, hard-boiled eggs and delicious pie. They had the window open, throwing out the chicken bones and other leavings. The concert company evidently had no dinner, and looked on with envy. The violinist said, licking his chops: "Hør, piger, det smager skam godt," (girls, you bet that tastes good.)

But pretty soon he noticed there was an awful draft from the window and said to the ladies: "I can jo not stand dot træk (draft)." And to the dinner party he said: "Vil you pleas luk dot vindow?" Yes, they all looked, but saw nothing unusual and went right on eating. Then he turned to his companions and said: "Now you can see, in America people do not understand dere own langvitch—dot is vot I alvays told you." His friends tried to tell him that he was not making himself understood, but he said: "Now you keep tight, I vil learn dose people someting—I piger holler med alle folk undtagen mei (you girls side with everybody but me)—Now I vil try it again."

So he leaned over and spoke to the mother of the lunchers again, saying: "Vil you kindly luk dot vindow."

They all looked at the window, but saw nothing startling, and went on eating. Turning to the ladies again he said: "Now you see, I have right—people here in Amerika do not unnerstan' der own langvitch. Nu skal I høre (now you shall hear): "I haf been all over Uropa, I haf been in Rusland, I haf been in France, I haf been in Germany and Belgium, but all over people unnerstands me because I speak de langvitch so immense perfect and plain—but here people unnerstand notting. But I vill ask her vun time more, but dot is also de last."

Then he leaned forward and said: "For de last time I ask you to luk dot vindow."

Of course they all looked again, eating great slices of bread as they did so. By this time, the violinist was so furious that he stood up and stretched across the woman's head, flattening her hat, and slammed the window down.

The conductor and passengers just roared with laughter, as they had been watching the little comedy. But his companions were disgusted with him, and one of the ladies said in Swedish: "Aa, fy hvor du er dum, jeg shems aa kjøra i hop med deg paa toget" (my, but you are stupid, I'm ashamed to be seen on the same train with you.) He sat and looked real hurt for a while, then he turned and said: "Men hør, piger, det var gælt. But dat vas wrong vot I said, 'luk dot vindow;' I should hav said, 'close dot vindow' "—and he seemed to enjoy the joke as much as anyone.

A NORWEGIAN WOMAN AT THE TELEPHONE

OH my, you must excuse me, I never use de telephone. Oh no, really I can't do it. You see I get so excita ven I yust look on it dat it ain't good for me—no really, I can't do it. You see I have took two bottles of Peruna, but dey don't do no good. I'm yust so nervous some I can be. Vell, I can try, but I don't like to do it.

Hel-lo, hel-lo! Oh, for goodness sake is it you, Lena? (tink, dat's my cousin)—I can't get over it, Lena, tink, I can hear you so good some if you should stand right here on de trap and talk to me. Oh, no, dat can't be. He don't drink—he's coming from better people in Norvay. Oh, de vife—yes, yes. Oh, for goodness sake, Lena, dat's de vorst I ever heard—de couldn't be anyvon could hear vot you is saying, could de? Oh my!

I vas down town yesterday—I vas on de town, "jeg var nær i byen"—you see my daughter is getting awfully long—she's getting big—de dresses are getting for kort (too short), and you see I can't use de same dresses for her every year, unless I put ruffles on dem. Oh, but you can tink I get a bargain, Lena—tink! I get lovely organdy. It vas fifteen cents a yard, men I get it for tirteen and tink! I get nuff ruffles for six dresses for eighteen cents; vasn't dat a bargain, Lena?

Hello Lena, hello— — —Lena,—vat's de matter, I didn't talk a nickle's vort. I can't hear anyting. Hello—oh, here she is. Lena, var vas you? Out in de kitchen and put on de koffee pot, I knew de vas someting, cause I couldn't hear anyting. Yes—I vas to de dentist. You see I got tree (3) teet up here and two down here and de dentist is going to take out all de old teet and put in new teet upstairs and downstairs for eight dollars. Isn't dat a bargain, Lena? You should really get new teet (teeth), de makes such a difference ven you smile. Say, Lena—can't you come over dis afternoon—Villie has got de whooping cough and ve is quarrantina, but you can come in de back vay.

"Oh, you know it's de hardest ting in de vorld for me to look sad."

A NORWEGIAN GIRL AT THE PHOTOGRAPHER

OH, how do you do. Is de photographer in? Oh, are you de picture man? Vell den, I spose I can tell you vat I vant. I vant to have my picture took, you see I left my yentleman frand in Norvay — tink of it, he's in Norvay and I haven't seen him for tree years. Tink, I haven't been in Norvay for tree years, isn't dat awful, and I vas yust tinking it vould be so nice to send him a picture of myself. Don't you tink dat vould be cute?

You know de trouble is, I vant to look real tin and you know dats a hard ting to do. Vould I look tinner if I stood dis vay or dis vay? And I vant de ring to show he gived me — vould it show if I stood like dis?

Oh, you know it's de hardest ting in de vorld for me to look sad, and I vant him to tink I been sad, all de time — ha ha ha ha ha ha! Don't take de picture now, I vant to look sad, vat — ha ha ha ha! I can't do it — I tink I'll die laughing.

O, really, it's so hard to feel sad — ha ha ha ha — vell, now I'm going to tink of de saddest tink I know — ha ha ha ha, vell really now, I'm going to try— . *(Poses).*

Oh, my — men I'm glad dats over — dats de hardest vork I ever did. Hurry dem up, von't you? Tank you, Mr. Photographer — I hope dere good.

A NORWEGIAN WOMAN AT THE BEACH
(With A Brood Of Erring Children)

NOW, Yoseph, don't you cause up any of dose monkeyshines you vas doing yesterday, or you can't go in de vater again dis veek. Aggie, don't pull your cap down like dat, Aggie. And remember, Aggie, you holding onto de rope. If you let go of de rope vun minute, you got to come in. Dick and Yonny, don't you pulling Aggie's feet from under her de vay you vas doing yesterday, or you can't go in de vater again dis veek. Hør du hva jeg sier til dig? Forstaar du at jeg mener business?

Oh, good morning, Mrs. Yones. Yes, de are a lovely day. Yes, I skud say de are a nice day. Children, you can go and play, but remember—de minute Mama calls you—come in. Hør du hva jeg sier til dig? Forstaar du at jeg mener business?

Say, here comes Miss Smitt. Dat's de tird badeing suit she's got on dis veek. Dey say she brought a trunk vit notting else but badeing suits in. Of kors, she never goes in de vater saa she don't get dem vet. Oh, I don't know. I don't tink she are saa pretty. De are someting about dat voman I don't like. And she's saa awful to talk. She's running around yust exactly like a millvheel. Oh yes, she's got a good figger. Her figger ain't saa bad. But anybody can have dat. You can see dat plain.

Dickie! Dickie! You hear Mama talking someting to you. You do dat vun time more and you got to come in.

Say, here comes Mrs. Yohnson. Vould you tink a voman vit a figger like dat vould go in de vater vit it. Oh my, isn't she tin. Oh, I skud say she are tin. Oh, she could be a nice enough voman. Jeg sier ikke noenting om det, forstaar du. But she has got de vorst children. I can't let my darlings play vit dem atall. And vat do you tink she has de nerve to say—dat I skud send my vunderful darlings to de reform school.

Yoseph! Yoseph! Oh, I don't dare look. Is dat my son Yoseph yumping off dat man's skulder? Aa jeg tør ikke se om han har kommet opp enda. It isn't Yoseph atall? It's vun of Mrs. Vallington's children? Vell, I vouldn't care if dey got good and drowned.

You see Dickie out dere anyver? *(shouts)* Dickie! Dickie! Can you see Dickie out dere? I vanted my children to vear Norvegian flags in dere hair saa I could tell dem apart in de vater, but dey von't do it.

Dickie, ver is Yonny? *(shouts)* Yonny! Yonny! Can you see Yonny out dere anyver? Oh gracious, I can't see him. Dickie, are you going to come in now? I'm not going to let dose children play in de vater anodder minute.

Aggie! Come in. Time is up. I don't believe in calling de children more dan vunce. Aggie! Forstaar du at jeg mener business? Yoseph! Dickie! Yonny! Are you going to come in here? Mama's calling you for de last time.

Ve had a very pleasant morning, didn't ve, Mrs. Yones.

PHOTOGRAPHS

FRONT COVER

Eleonora Olson in costume. *1924*

FRONTISPIECE

Victor Records Poster *1924*

CENTER SECTION

Pages 1, 2, 7, & 8

Eleonora Olson Concert Trio Program *1910-1911 Season*

Page 6

Eleonora and Ethel Olson in Songs and Readings *year unknown*

Pages 3, 4, & 5

a. Eleonora Olson (at far right) in a singing group. *1880's*
b. Ethel Olson *about 1897*
c. Eleonora Olson in the Norwegian national costume. *about 1900*
d. The Magnus Quartette *1904* left to right: Helen Watson, Blanche Hattersly, Louise Lake, Ethel Olson.
e. Ethel Olson *about 1905*
f. Mrs. Dikka Koren's boarding house *about 1919* left to right: Herbjørn Gausta, Eleonora Olson, Dikka Koren, Jacob Preus, Erling Hvoslev, Olav Coll, Ethel Olson, — — — — Hvoslev.
g. Eleonora (left) and Ethel (right) with their mother, Johanna. *about 1905*
h. Ethel Olson *1910*
i. Eleonora Olson *1910*
j. Left to right: J.A.O. Preus, Ethel Olson, Olav Coll, Eleonora Olson. *about 1906*
k. The Eleonora Olson Concert Trio *about 1910* left to right: pianist Alice Walden, Eleonora, Ethel.

l. The Eleonora Olson Concert Company *1915* left to right: pianist Ivy Berry, Eleonora, Ethel.
m. The Olson Sisters *1924* Ethel (sitting) and Eleonora (standing).

BACK COVER

The Skovgaard Concert Company *1905* Axel Skovgaard, Christine Nilsson, Eleonora Olson.

The Olson Sisters Concert Company *1920*

IMPORTANT DATES

1846 Johanna, the mother of Eleonora and Ethel, is born in Hafslo Indre Sogn, Norway.

1860 Johanna and her parents, Gjert and Malene Anderson Dahlen, emigrate and settle in Koshkonung, Wisconsin.

1865 Johanna marries Otto Olson Bing in Chicago.

1870 Their daughter, Eleonora Mathilda, is born.

1889 Their daughter, Ethel Christine, is born.

1899 Otto Olson Bing is killed in an accident while working as a railroad guard in Leadville, Colorado.

1905 Eleonora joins the Skovgaard Concert Company in St. Paul.

1909 Eleonora and Ethel form their own concert company.

1920 The sisters start recording on the Victor label.

1923 Ethel marries Dr. R. M. Pederson in Minneapolis. The Olson Sisters stop touring.

1925 First edition of *Yust For Fun* appears.

1929 Second edition of *Yust For Fun*.

1933 Johanna Olson Bing dies.

1943 Ethel dies.

1944 Dr. Pederson dies.

1946 Eleonora dies.

DISCOGRAPHY

Edison Records — These were perhaps the earliest recordings done by the Olson Sisters. No titles are known.

Victor Records — See the frontispiece of this book. The comic monologues were in English with the exception of **Kaffeslabberas**. The songs were all in Norwegian.

Brunswick Records — By Ethel: **Story Of The Bookcase, The Ball Game, A Norwegian Woman At The Telephone, Laughing Record, Preparations For Mabel's Wedding.**

By Eleonora: **Sogne Kjerring** (The Old Sogning Woman), **Aa, Ola, Ola, Min Eigen Onge** (Oh, Ole, Ole, I Loved You Dearly), **Og Jeg Vil Ha Mig En Hjaertenskiaer** (I Want A Sweetheart) from "Til Saeters".

Four of Ethel's monologues appear to duplicate her Victor recordings; the titles are nearly identical. **Preparations For Mabel's Wedding** is listed only in the Brunswick catalog. The monologue by Eleonora is probably in Norwegian as are her two songs.